I never would have guessed in a hundred lifetimes that I would have found the one person I consider to be the perfect soul mate for me.

But I have found you. And it's like finding out that miracles really do happen and dreams...
really can come true.

— Casey Whilson

Blue Mountain Arts®

Bestselling Titles

By Susan Polis Schutz:
To My Daughter with Love on the Important Things in Life
To My Son with Love

By Douglas Pagels:
30 Beautiful Things That Are True About You
42 Gifts I'd Like to Give to You
100 Things to Always Remember... and One Thing to Never Forget
May You Always Have an Angel by Your Side
To the One Person I Consider to Be My Soul Mate

By Donna Fargo:
I Prayed for You Today
To the Love of My Life

52 Lessons on Communicating Love
by Dr. Ruth Westheimer

Is It Time to Make a Change?
by Deanna Beisser

Anthologies:
7 Days to a Positive Attitude
Always Believe in Yourself and Your Dreams
For You, My Daughter
Friends for Life
Hang In There
I Love You, Mom
I'm Glad You Are My Sister
The Joys and Challenges of Motherhood
The Language of Recovery
Marriage Is a Promise of Love
Teaching and Learning Are Lifelong Journeys
There Is Greatness Within You, My Son
Think Positive Thoughts Every Day
Thoughts to Share with a Wonderful Teenager
True Wealth
With God by Your Side ...You Never Have to Be Alone
You're Just like a Sister to Me

To My
Soul Mate

Words to Share
with the Love
of a Lifetime

Edited by Gary Morris

Blue Mountain Press ®

Boulder, Colorado

We wish to thank Susan Polis Schutz for permission to reprint the following poems that appear in this publication: "Love," "I Love You More Than 'Love'," "I Promise That I Will Love You," "For So Many Reasons...," "I Love You," "Love can make you feel like...," "You Are My World, You Are My Love," "I can't believe it...," and "You're Still the One." Copyright © 1982, 1986, 1989, 1990, 1991, 2006 by Stephen Schutz and Susan Polis Schutz. And for "With My Love Come These Promises...." Copyright © 1979 by Continental Publications. All rights reserved.

Library of Congress Control Number: 2006902824
ISBN-13: 978-1-59842-171-2
ISBN-10: 1-59842-171-9

ACKNOWLEDGMENTS appear on page 80.

Certain trademarks are used under license.
BLUE MOUNTAIN PRESS is registered in U.S. Patent and Trademark Office.

Manufactured in China.

 This book is printed on recycled paper.

This book is printed on fine quality, laid embossed, 80 lb. paper. This paper has been specially produced to be acid free (neutral pH) and contains no groundwood or unbleached pulp. It conforms with all the requirements of the American National Standards Institute, Inc., so as to ensure that this book will last and be enjoyed by future generations.

Blue Mountain Arts, Inc.

P.O. Box 4549, Boulder, Colorado 80306

Contents

To the Love of My Life

How many ways can I say I love you and still make you smile?

I'll cross my fingers that whether or not my words measure up, you'll at least know that you and you alone hold the key to my heart.

I love you for your thoughtfulness and tenderness, for always being so good to me, for your easy attitude, your faithfulness and loyalty, and your commitment to us. I love you because you let me be who I am, because you want the best for me, and because you love me, too… I want to be everything to you that you are to me.

Does this sound like I love you, that I'm smitten to the core, and that no one could ever take your place?

I just know this… as long as my heart beats, I will love you — my partner, the love of my life, and my best friend. No matter what happens, I'll be just fine as long as you are my roommate in this place called life.

— *Donna Fargo*

Have I Told You Lately That I Love You?

Have I told you lately that seeing your face at the end of the day makes all the hard work and struggle worthwhile? That cuddling with you in front of the TV at the end of the night is the best part of my day (closely followed by waking next to you each morning)?

Have I told you lately that I thank my lucky stars we met? That I can't believe how right our relationship feels? That I can't imagine two people on this earth who were meant to be together more than you and I?

Have I told you lately that I'd rather spend time with you than anyone else? That no matter how much time we spend together, it will never be enough? That wrapped in your arms is the safest, nicest place there is?

Have I told you lately that just thinking about you makes me want to burst with happiness? That looking at your picture or hearing your voice still makes my heart skip a beat? That I still find our relationship surprising and exciting and deeply satisfying?

Have I told you lately that I love you? Well, I do. And whether I remember to tell you every day or not, I love you and I always will.

— *Donna Gephart*

I Hope You Know...

Sometimes I get so caught up
in my own busy world
that I forget what means the most
to me in my life.
I get so wrapped up
that I let too much time go by
without telling you that you
mean absolutely everything to me.

When I'm not with you,
I'm thinking of you.
When I don't know where you are,
I'm worrying about you.
And when I am with you...
I wonder how I could let
any time at all go by
without telling you
how much I love you.

— *Traci-Delores Anderson*

I'm So Lucky to Have Found You

Once in a lifetime,
    you find someone
who touches not only your heart,
    but also your soul.
You discover someone
who stands beside you,
    not over you.
You find someone
who loves you for who you are,
    and not for who you could be.
Once in a lifetime,
    if you're lucky,
you find someone…
    as I have found you.

— *Nanci Brillant*

Do You Know
When I First
Fell in Love with You?

I remember the first time you touched me.
It was then I gave you my heart.
In that moment, my life changed.
Falling in love with you was like being
first to discover the most beautiful
    thing in the world
or to find something so lovely
that no one else had ever noticed.
It was like glimpsing the first
    evening star
or the rainbow that unexpectedly
appears in the midst of a storm.

Love often starts in little ways.
It comes quietly with a smile,
    a glance, or a touch,
but you know it's there
because suddenly you're not alone
and the sadness inside you is gone.
Love means finally finding a place
    in this world that shelters you
and is your very own —
where you feel you have been forever
and you live and grow and learn.
You did all this with your touch…
and every time you touch me,
I fall in love with you all over again.

— *Vickie M. Worsham*

Sometimes I look at you and find myself remembering the first time we kissed, the first time you said "I love you," and the first time I realized I wanted to spend the rest of my life with you. Every time I look back on those days, I'm so happy to realize that even after everything we've been through since then — all the fights and the difficulties we've faced — I still want to be with you forever.

— *Rachyl Taylor*

If You Ever Wonder How I Feel About You...

Look in the mirror.
In your reflection you'll see…
the person I want to spend
my whole life with,
the one I love more than
    words can say,
the one who makes me happy,
the one I want to grow
    old with.
So if you ever have any
doubt about who makes
my life complete, look into
the mirror and you'll see.
I love you…
today and always.

— *Jason Blume*

This Is Why
We Belong Together...

Because whenever
    you smile,
something deep inside me
urges me to smile back;
whenever I'm down
and I hear your laughter,
I come alive again.
Whenever I get too excited or agitated,
you know how to calm me down.
I often catch myself
watching your face as you talk
or when you listen to others,
and just seeing your reactions
    makes me happy.

I know we belong together because
when we talk you'll say something
that has been asleep in me for a while,
or even something I never knew was there.
You're the first person
I want to see in the morning
and the last one I want to touch
before I go to sleep.
You're the one I want to turn to
when things get rough;
the one I want to share
my happiness with
when things are going great;
the one to whom I want to entrust
my dreams and my heart.
I have a faith in you
unlike the faith I have in anyone else,
because you bring out the best in me,
just as I bring it out in you.

I know we belong together because
I want to love you
and do for you all that love entails.
I want your happiness as much as
I want my own, if not more,
and this desire will never go away.

— *Christine Nemec*

For So Many Reasons...
I Love You

I love you
for being so honest
for being so free
for being so trusting
for being so passionate
and for contributing so much
to our relationship

I love you soooo much. I love you soooo much.

I love you
for all you do for me
for all you express to me
for all you share with me
and for all that you are

I love you
for understanding me
for laughing and crying
with me
for having fun with me
and for being such
an outstanding person

I love you
for being so strong
for being so independent
for being so creative
and for being such a unique person

I love you
for all these things and more
I love you
for everything about you

I love you

— *Susan Polis Schutz*

I Am So Touched by All That I Share with You...

I never would have guessed in a
hundred lifetimes that I would have
found the one person I consider to be
the perfect soul mate for me.

But I have found you. And it's like
finding out that miracles really do
happen and dreams...
     really can come true.
I am so deeply and so endlessly in
love with you.

Sometimes I can't imagine that I could
possibly care more than I already do.
But then... you do something wonderful.
Or you just look at me in a way that lets
me see how real our love is. Or you
surprise me with the sweetest, most
enfolding hug I've ever had. Or a long
and lingering kiss...

And the next thing I know, my heart has grown even bigger than it was before. It's almost like my happiness gently knocks on the door and says "We need to make more room inside. I've got so many smiles and hopes and memories that need a place to stay, and there are so many more where these came from."

And it's always the same; my heart is so thankful that the visitor is you... that it would do anything to hold on to the treasures of those joys. I don't know if anyone else will ever understand how much I love you... but I really hope <u>you</u> do.

— *Casey Whilson*

$\mathcal{W}$e've been through
So much together
Sometimes it feels like
We've known each other
From the very beginning
Sometimes I feel like
Our souls were connected
On a special level
Before we ever
Actually met

— *Regina Hill*

soul mates soul mates soul mates soul mates soul mates soul mates soul mates soul mates soul mates soul mates soul mates soul mates soul mates

A Soul Mate Is Someone Who...

- will watch you while you sleep
- will kiss you out of a bad dream
- will laugh, cry, and share with you
- will celebrate with you
- will cherish every feeling you experience
- will be grateful that you're you
- will whisper sweet somethings in your ear
- will encourage you to follow your dreams
- will always be on your side
- will love you unconditionally

A soul mate is someone who...

is everything you are to me!

— *Miranda Moti*

"Why I Love You So Much"

Once upon a time, long ago, I made a wish.
A really nice person is all I asked for.
But...

An incredibly wonderful love is what I got! I'm still
    trying to figure out how I managed to be so lucky!

I think that some people spend half their lives making
    those kinds of wishes... and the other half trying to
    find their place in the world. I'm so glad I found the
    right place... at the right time... with the right person.

My favorite thing in the entire universe is... just to be
    sitting across from you, looking in your eyes, talking
    about anything and everything, and feeling so
    wonderful inside.
It's holding your hand and walking anywhere the
    afternoon takes us. It's laughing so easily and trusting
    so completely.
It's watching the sun go down and the stars come into
    view and just feeling that, in the grand scheme of
    things, nothing could possibly be sweeter... than
    having you here.

It's closing my eyes and looking forward to all the joys tomorrow will bring... and thinking about so many different things. Like sharing a home. Being the happiest family. And making the best memories anyone has ever made.

It's living our daily lives as two individuals and dealing with all the demands of the day, but always finding a hug to come home to.
It's cuddling up close. It's feeling so good and knowing that what we have is so right.

It's two hearts that are a million times happier together than they could ever be alone.
It's turning a fantasy and a wish into a "happily-ever-after" dream... come true.

It's having a favorite place in the world and knowing that it's...

wherever I am

as long as I'm with you.

— *Chris Gallatin*

You Are My World,
You Are My Love

What if we had never met?
What would I be doing?
What kind of life would I have?
I often think about these things
and I always come to
   the same conclusion

You Are My World*You Are My World*

*You Are My World*You Are My World*

Without you
I would be an extremely
    unhappy person
living an unhappy life
I know that we met for a reason
and that reason was that
you and I were meant to be
in love with each other
You and I were meant to be
a team giving us strength
to function happily in the world
I am so thankful that things
turned out the way they did
and we were brought together
You are my world
You are my love

— *Susan Polis Schutz*

No Matter What...
I Love You

Despite any obstacles that
    come our way
and all the many differences
    we've shared,
I find myself loving you more
    with time.

I love you when our moods vary
and when our opinions go
    in opposite directions.
I love you when your ideas
    aren't quite the same as mine
        and our beliefs clash.
I love you when you take a stand
    on what you feel is absolutely right,
even if I don't feel the same way.
I even love you when you're tired
    and grumpy
and don't want much to do with me
    at that moment.

What I'm trying to say is that
   I love you no matter what,
even as we struggle to be
   our own individuals.
It doesn't matter how different
   we may be.
As I've spent more and more time
   by your side,
I've learned that I love you most of all
   because you are different from me
     and can express it.

I love you for what you believe,
   for the emotions you feel,
and for the ideas that help me
   open my own mind
to possibilities I haven't yet explored.

— Beverly K. Metott

$\mathcal{L}$ove doesn't mean that you will never feel pain or that you'll live a life free from care. It doesn't mean that you will never be hurt or that your life will be perfect, with every moment consumed by happiness.

Love does mean that you will always have a companion, someone to help you through the difficult times and rejoice with you in your times of celebration. It means that each argument is followed by a time of forgiveness, and each time of sorrow is far outweighed by all the tender moments spent in each other's arms.

— *Michele Weber*

I'll Never Give Up on Us

Perfect love only happens
    in the movies.

In the real world we sometimes
    say things in anger
that we wish we could take back.
We sometimes do foolish things —
without thinking about the consequences…
and we hurt the ones we love most.
But that doesn't mean our love isn't real —
or that it's not worth fighting for.

Let's focus on what's good between us
and remember the reasons why
    love brought us together.

I believe we can grow
    from these hard times
and our relationship
will become stronger and healthier
as we learn more about
the power of compromise,
    forgiveness —
        and love.

— *Jason Blume*

You Are What I Long For

J long to awaken next to you,
to hear you say my name,
to kiss you first thing in the morning,
to begin my day with you,
and to tell you over and over again
that I love you.

I long to look into your eyes,
to hold your hand in mine,
to have a little laugh with you,
to go out into the world with you,
and to tell you over and over again
that I love you.

I long to sit beside you,
to see your sweet smile,
to learn something new about you,
to spend my whole day with you,
and to tell you over and over again
that I love you.

I long to go home with you,
to relax and have fun with you,
to say thanks for what we have shared,
to end my day with you,
and to tell you over and over again
that I love you.

I long to have you in my arms,
to hold you tight against me,
to kiss you last thing in the evening,
to begin my night with you,
and to tell you over and over again
that I love you.

— *Gregory E. Lang*

I Love You

Sometimes I worry about you
You don't relax enough
You work so hard
There is so much for you to do

Sometimes I worry about you
You don't realize how much
    you are appreciated
or how much you give of yourself
    to others

I Love You I Love You I Love You

I Love You I Love You I Love You I Love You

But I am thankful
for the way you are
as I realize it is the
only way you could be

And at all times I want you
    to know
that I respect you so greatly
and I thank you for
being wonderful
in every way
I love you

— *Susan Polis Schutz*

A Loving Thought About the Person I Want to Be ...for You

J want to be someone who reminds you every single day how much you're loved. I want to be someone who makes you happy.

I want to be someone you can trust. With absolutely everything. Every feeling you feel like sharing. Every hope and worry. Every joy. Every sorrow. I want to be the one person in the universe you know you can always turn to. Someone you can laugh with whenever you want to, cry with if you ever need to, and just be yourself with... anytime. I want to be the one thing you're sure about.

I want to be someone who makes you smile a million times more than I make you frown. I want to make beautiful memories with you. I want to go so many places with you. I want to see more sunsets with you than I could even begin to count. I want to sit across from you at dinner. I want to talk about the day. I want to hold you and walk with you and say a quiet thanks for you as many times as I possibly can... in my time on this earth.

I want to be a part of your tomorrows. I want you to be a part of every one of mine. And more than anything else,
    I want to be what you think of...

        every time
            you think of happiness
                and forever
                    and love.

— Chris Gallatin

True love is being the best of friends — being able to say and share anything while still being sensitive to the other's feelings.

It is knowing that life will bring pain and sorrow, but together, you will support each other and overcome even the most difficult times.

True love is showing and saying "I love you" even when you both know — through a simple smile — that doing so isn't necessary.

True love is complete within itself, and it lasts into eternity.

— *Tim Tweedie*

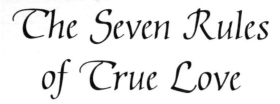

The Seven Rules of True Love

1. Love yourself. If you love yourself you will automatically be good to yourself and others.
2. Put the needs of others first. When you love someone else, tune in to their personal needs, growth, and development. Your love will be like sunshine for a plant, like wind for the waves.
3. Be prepared to sacrifice. Love is not always rainbows and butterflies. Sometimes, even love requires us to nourish, develop, and work at it.
4. Communicate. Honest communication is the foundation of real love.
5. Forgive. No one is perfect 100 percent of the time.
6. Spend time with your loved ones.
7. Love unconditionally. This is real love which never dies. The sun never sets on true love.

— *Milton Willis and Michael Willis*

Love

Love is being happy for the other person
  when that person is happy
  being sad for the other person
  when that person is sad
  being together in good times
  and being together in bad times
Love is the source of strength

Love is being honest with yourself at all times
  being honest with the other person at all times
  telling, listening, respecting the truth
  and never pretending
Love is the source of reality

Love is an understanding so complete that
  you feel as if you are a part of the other person
  accepting that person just the way he or she is
  and not trying to change each other
  to be something else
Love is the source of unity

Love is the freedom to pursue your own desires
  while sharing your experiences with the other person
  the growth of one individual alongside of
  and together with the growth
  of another individual
Love is the source of success

Love is the excitement of planning things together
  the excitement of doing things together
Love is the source of the future

Love is the fury of the storm
  the calm in the rainbow
Love is the source of passion

Love is giving and taking in a daily situation
  being patient with each other's needs and desires
Love is the source of sharing

Love is knowing that the other person
  will always be with you
  regardless of what happens
  missing the other person when he or she is away
  but remaining near in heart at all times
Love is the source of security

Love is the source of life

— Susan Polis Schutz

You

You have the kind of face
I could fall in love with
And I did

You have the kind of lips
I would love to kiss
And I do

You have the kind of mind
I can admire and respect
And I will

You have the kind of body
That I find attractive and desire
And I have

You have a sense of humor
That makes me laugh each day
And it does

You have a sense of honor
I know I can depend on
And I will

You have the kind of heart
That makes the world a better place
And it does

You are the kind of person
I could love forevermore
And I shall

— David Jay Bernstein

A Wish Filled with Love Just for You...

I wish for your heart to always
   be loved,
your hand to be held,
and your voice to be heard.

I wish for your prayers to always
   be answered,
your secrets to be kept,
and your dreams to come true.

I wish for your desires to always
   be fulfilled,
your beliefs to be spoken,
and your generosity to be appreciated.

I wish for your kindness to always
    be returned,
your trust to never be broken,
and your happiness to never end.

I wish for your courage to always
    be strong,
your pride to never be hurt,
and your challenges
    to be conquered.

I wish for your life to always
    be treasured...
and your treasure to always be life.
I wish for you to always feel
    deeply loved...
because you are.

— *Danelle Mighton*

It Must Be Love

*W*hat else can you call it, this sweet,
delicious thing that lives between us?
We get hopelessly lost in it, only to
rediscover ourselves along the way.
Bigger than both of us and deep as an
ocean, it must be love.

Love sneaks up on us when we're
looking in some other direction. We can
fall in love, become wrapped up in love,
or be wonderfully, foolishly, taken by
love. And whatever storms we weather,
one thing always stands true: it must be
love, shared by me and you.

I love you so very much.

— *Rachel Snyder*

With My Love
Come These Promises...

J will support you
in all that you
do
I will help you
in all that you
need
I will share with you
in all that you
experience
I will encourage you
in all that you
try
I will understand you
in all that is in your
heart
I will love you
in all that you
are

— *Susan Polis Schutz*

I Love You This Much...

Enough to do anything for you — give my life,
  my love, my heart, and my soul to you and
  for you.
Enough to give all my time, efforts, thoughts,
  talents, trust, and prayers willingly to you.
Enough to want to protect you, care for you,
  guide you, hold you, comfort you, listen to
  you, and cry to you and with you.
Enough to be completely comfortable with you,
  act silly around you, never have to hide
  anything from you, and be myself with you.
Enough to share all my sentiments, dreams,
  goals, fears, hopes, and worries — my entire
  life with you.
Enough to want the best for you, to wish for your
  successes, and to hope for the fulfillment of
  all your endeavors.
Enough to keep my promises to you and pledge
  my loyalty and faithfulness to you.

Enough to cherish your friendship, adore your
personality, respect your values, and see
you for who you are.
Enough to fight for you, compromise for you,
and sacrifice myself for you if need be.
Enough to miss you incredibly when we're
apart, no matter what length of time it's for
and regardless of the distance.
Enough to believe in our relationship, to stand
by it through the worst of times, to have
faith in our strength as a couple, and to
never give up on us.
Enough to spend the rest of my life with you,
be there for you when you need or want
me, and never, ever want to leave you or
live without you.

I love you this much.

— *Lisa M. Thomas*

$\mathcal{A}$ true relationship
knows of but one great thing:
to give of one's self
boundlessly
in order to find one's self
richer,
deeper,
better.

— *Emma Goldman*

$\mathcal{J}$ can't believe it
Out of all the millions of people
in hundreds of countries
and thousands of cities
I was able to find
my true heart
my true soul
my true love

Everyone searches for love
Love unites our hearts
I love you

— *Susan Polis Schutz*

If I Could Give You Just One Thing…

It would be my heart —
full of love for you…

If I could give you everything…
each day, I would bring you
a bundle of cream-colored roses
and sprinkle the soft petals
to make a bed for you.
I would cause the murmur
of a steady rain and distant thunder
to lull you toward sweet slumber.
I would lay a carpet of new grass
beneath your feet
for you to sit upon and daydream
in the shade of a tree that always
gave you the colors of fall.

I would bring you the ocean waves
and chase away from you
the harsh rays of the sun.
I would capture a full moon for you
and pray that I would always know
what your heart desires.

If I could give you everything,
I would do all this for you.
But if I could give you just *one thing*…
I would give you my heart,
because it belongs to no one else
and it is filled with love for you.

— *Gregory E. Lang*

$\mathcal{I}$'m a little bit more
in love with you
each morning
when I wake up.
I'm a little bit more
in love with you
every time
you say my name.
I'm a little bit more
in love with you
every time
you walk into the room...

I'm a little bit more
in love with you
every day.

— *Ashley Rice*

Love can make you feel like
the most important person on earth
in a world of billions of people
It is the emotion that wakes
your senses to see the beauty
of the sun setting
the flowers blooming
the snow melting
It is the feeling behind
all tears and laughter
It is the feeling of all feelings

— *Susan Polis Schutz*

I Just Want to Remind You How Much I Appreciate You!

Too many times it seems we take for granted the ones we love. We wait for birthdays or holidays or some other special occasion to say "I love you," "I appreciate you," or "thank you." We let life carry us away on a never-ending road filled with the responsibilities of a day-to-day existence.

In our busy lives, we often forget that there is more along the way than just bills to pay, phone calls to return, and errands to run. There are people in our lives who need to be hugged, who need to be loved. There are people in our lives who need their accomplishments noticed and praised.

We need to remember how fragile hearts can be, how quickly a soul can grow weary, how fast a spirit can break.

Forgive me for forgetting that a heart is like a garden that needs to be tended to and nourished with what only another heart can give — love and appreciation, devotion and honesty.

Thank you for loving me and for putting up with me. I appreciate you not only for what you have done, but for what you have become and what we are together. I'm proud of you, and I'm proud to be with you.

Even when the road of life becomes a little too curvy or a little too long, I love you, and I want you to always remember that.

— Tracia Gloudemans

$\mathcal{A}$s often as I've heard you say,
  "I love you,"
I never tire of hearing
  those three words —
just as I never tire of saying them.
I never stop appreciating
your honesty, sensitivity,
thoughtfulness, or generosity.
Most of all,
as often as I'm with you,
I never stop appreciating
  what we have together
or what a blessing it is
to have you in my life.

— Lynda Schab

$\mathcal{L}$ove is a short word but it contains everything. Love means the body, the soul, the life, the entire being. We feel love as we feel the warmth of our blood, we breathe love as we breathe the air, we hold it in ourselves as we hold our thoughts. Nothing more exists for us. Love is not a word; it is a wordless state indicated by four letters.

— *Guy de Maupassant*

One word frees us of all
the weight and pain of life:
that word is love.

— *Sophocles*

I Love You
More Than "Love"

It is impossible to capture in words
the feelings I have for you
They are the strongest feelings that I
have ever had about anything
yet when I try to tell you them
or try to write them to you
the words do not even begin to touch
the depths of my feelings
And though I cannot explain the essence of
these phenomenal feelings
I can tell you what I feel like
    when I am with you
When I am with you it is as if
    I were a bird
        flying freely in the clear blue sky
When I am with you it is as if
    I were a flower
        opening up my petals of life

When I am with you it is as if
   I were the waves of the ocean
      crashing strongly against the shore
When I am with you it is as if
   I were the rainbow after the storm
      proudly showing my colors
When I am with you it is as if
   everything that is beautiful
      surrounds us
This is just a very small part of how wonderful
I feel when I am with you
Maybe the word "love" was invented to explain
the deep, all-encompassing feelings
   that I have for you
but somehow it is not strong enough
But since it is the best word that there is
let me tell you a thousand times that
I love you more than
"love"

            — *Susan Polis Schutz*

Love is always being there for each other with a shoulder to cry on, to give support when confidence levels are low, to give helpful advice when it is asked for, to know when to be silent and just listen, or to give cheerful words of encouragement. It is sharing the good and the bad, the hopes and the dreams, the amusing times and the serious times. It is doing things together, yet leaving room for each to grow as an individual.

— *Beverly Bruce*

In My Heart

You don't have to be perfect to belong in this place. You don't have to have all the answers or always know the right thing to say. You can climb the highest mountain if you want. Or quietly imagine that you might someday. You can take chances or take safety nets, make miracles or make mistakes. You don't have to be composed at all hours to be strong here. You don't have to be bold or certain to be brave. You don't have to have all the answers here or even know who you want to be...

Just take my hand and rest your heart and stay awhile with me.

— Ashley Rice

When I Look in Your Eyes...

J see all the things that you are —
kindness, gentleness, compassion, and love.

There's a twinkle that sometimes appears
when you are talking about
the beautiful things in this world
that are so important to you.

When I hear your voice...
I hear the sweetest sound
I have ever heard.
When you say, "I love you,"
it touches me in a way no other words
ever have or ever will touch me again.

When I see your face...
I see someone who has so much depth.
Your face reflects a bittersweet past
and holds so much hope for the future.

It's an honest and trusting face,
   with a youthful quality
that is so rare in a world that makes us
   grow old before our time.

When you hold me...
you have a way like magic
of making me feel so peaceful, secure,
and content with my world
   and everything that is around me.
Life is a wonderland in your arms —
a place I thought I would never find.

When you love me...
that is the greatest gift of all.
You give me an unselfish, undemanding,
   uninhibited kind of love
that I thought only existed
   in my dreams.
You have filled an empty space inside me,
and now I feel that I am complete.

Your love has given me life,
and now, with you, my life is full of love.

— *Marianne Freeman*

You Are the Love
of a Lifetime
I've Always Wanted
as Mine...

...and You Are the
Special Soul Mate
I Always Hoped
I'd Find

Love of My Life Love of My Life Love of My Life

$\mathcal{I}$ can barely begin to tell you how much I value the exquisite closeness that we have been given. It is a truly beautiful blessing. And there will never be a day when I will take even one moment of that joy and that sweetness for granted. I know what
a gift you are…

I want you to know it, too.

You have an amazing way of touching my heart, and you have a way of turning every day into a time and a place where the nicest feelings and the deepest gratitude all come together.

I have such an immense amount of thanks and appreciation for all this.

And if it's okay with you…
I'd love to go on loving you

forever.

— *L. N. Mallory*

I Want You Beside Me Always

I want to grow old with you,
lose count of the sunsets we share,
stroll along a moonlit beach —
always holding hands and looking into
each other's eyes with deep longing —
no matter our age.
I want memories of sitting by a campfire,
warm conversation filling the
crisp forest air between us,
and evening whispers among the trees
filling my soul with love for you.
I want to wake beside you each morning
and feel the brightness and warmth
of your sunshine on my face.
I want to travel the world
with you beside me,
explore the space between our souls,
and feel the ever-growing love
that feeds our spirits.

I want to feel the universe between us,
sit beneath the clear evening sky,
imagine heaven, and thank God for
the gift of you.
I want to play in the snow,
make angels, and write messages of love
with my gloved hand.
I want to face the challenge of conveying
to you this deepening love I have.
Trying to tell you how much
I love you is like translating
beautiful music into something
that is still and silent —
yet I shall always make the effort,
though it seems as impossible as
describing heaven.

I want you beside me
as my best friend and lover.
Always.
I want you forever with me,
forever soul mates,
today and always…
beyond tomorrow.

— *Tim M. Krzys*

$\mathcal{L}$et us always love
each other more and more
as long as life lasts
and make each other
happier every year.

— *George Eliot*

You're Still the One

After all this time
I still want to be with you
    more than with anyone else
I still want to talk to you
    before anyone else
I still want to
laugh with you
walk with you
read with you
play with you
be quiet with you
be noisy with you
make plans with you
discuss the past and future with you

After all this time
you are still the person who makes me
    happy, content, excited and peaceful
And after all this time
our love not only prevails
but is stronger than ever

— *Susan Polis Schutz*

A Daily Reminder for the One I Love

We say "I love you"
   just about every day.
Sometimes the words are whispered
   as we fall asleep at night;
sometimes they're spoken at the end
   of a phone conversation
or accompanied by a quick kiss
   as we rush out the door.
The words are always there,
but sometimes we forget to think about
how much they really mean.

Every time you hear me say
   those three little words,
I want you to remember that
   they're coming from the bottom
   of my heart.

I want you to remember that I love you
   for everything you are
and for everything I am with you.
I want you to remember that you're
   the best person I've ever known
and I feel so lucky to have you in my life.

I want you to remember that true love
   is forever
and there is no love truer than
   the love I feel for you.
I want you to remember that you're
   the most wonderful thing
      that has ever happened to me,
my happy ending,
my dream come true,
my friend and my love
   all wrapped up in one.

I love you.

             — *Rachyl Taylor*

4 Things I Look Forward to Doing with You

I want to walk life's path with you by my side. I want us to be together, because I love you and because being with you seems more meant to be than anything that's ever happened to me. In the course of our time together, you have filled my heart with more hope and joy than I ever knew I could be blessed with.

I want to go places with you. I want us to set off to see what's at the end of every rainbow. But we don't have to go adventuring miles and miles away. There's a lot to see right here, close to home. Close to you. And having you close to me. I want us to explore the special things, the feelings we have for one another, and I want us to discover that the single best place in the world is wherever we are… when we're together.

I want us to have a deeper and sweeter understanding than we've ever known before. I want us to talk things over, whether they're little or large, and say all the things that we want to share. I don't ever want us to worry about whether it's okay or not, or whether we have to filter things out. I want us to have a direct connection, heart to heart, and to have the open, easy, caring kind of communication that keeps people so close and makes them so happy inside. And...

> I want to love you
> for the rest
> of my life.

— *Marta Best*

I Love You
Soooo Much

You have so many things no one else
    will ever have.
You have all my love — now and forever.
You have my admiration — for being such
    an incredibly precious person.
You have my unending gratitude — for the way
    you brighten my life.
You have my hopes — all gently hoping you
    know how glad I am that you warmed my
    world and touched my very soul.

You have my every affection.
You have my desires and dreams.
You even have things there are no words for.
You have whispered words that belong to you,
    thoughts you have inspired, and blessings that
    have touched the deepest part of my heart.
You have the most beautiful wishes the stars
    and I can wish, and my prayer that someday
      I'll be able to thank you for all this.

You have a standing invitation to share the
days with me — and to be the one and
only person who holds the key to my
happiness.
You have arms I want around me, eyes
I want to lose myself in, and a joy in
your voice that I could listen to forever.

You have empty pages in the story of your
life — pages I'd like us to write together…
filling them with memories we'll make
and stories that will travel beside us
and carry us over whatever comes along.

You have my sweet appreciation — for taking
my smiles places that my heart has only
dreamed of.

And you'll always have me,
my "thank-God-for-you" feelings,
and soooo much love.

— *Marin McKay*

I Promise
That I Will Love You

I cannot promise you that
I will not change
I cannot promise you that
I will not have many different moods
I cannot promise you that
I will not hurt your feelings sometimes
I cannot promise you that
I will not be erratic
I cannot promise you that
I will always be strong
I cannot promise you that
my faults will not show

But —
I do promise you that
I will always be supportive of you
I do promise you that
I will share all my thoughts
    and feelings with you
I do promise you that
I will give you freedom to be yourself
I do promise you that
I will understand everything that you do
I do promise you that
I will be completely honest with you
I do promise you that
I will laugh and cry with you
I do promise you that
I will help you achieve all your goals
But —
    most of all
        I do promise you that
        I will love you

— *Susan Polis Schutz*

ACKNOWLEDGMENTS

We gratefully acknowledge the permission granted by the following authors and authors' representatives to reprint poems or excerpts from their publications.

PrimaDonna Entertainment Corp. for "To the Love of My Life" by Donna Fargo. Copyright © 2006 by PrimaDonna Entertainment Corp. All rights reserved.

Jason Blume for "If You Ever Wonder How I Feel About You..." and "I'll Never Give Up on Us." Copyright © 2004, 2005 by Jason Blume. All rights reserved.

Gregory E. Lang for "You Are What I Long For" and "If I Could Give You Just One Thing...." Copyright © 2006 by Gregory E. Lang. All rights reserved.

Milton Willis and Michael Willis for "The Seven Rules of True Love." Copyright © 2006 by Milton Willis and Michael Willis. All rights reserved.

Rachel Snyder for "It Must Be Love." Copyright © 2006 by Rachel Snyder. All rights reserved.

A careful effort has been made to trace the ownership of selections used in this anthology in order to obtain permission to reprint copyrighted material and give proper credit to the copyright owners. If any error or omission has occurred, it is completely inadvertent, and we would like to make corrections in future editions provided that written notification is made to the publisher:

BLUE MOUNTAIN ARTS, INC., P.O. Box 4549, Boulder, Colorado 80306.